TACKLING IT WITH TEENAGERS

By Adrienne Katz

With research by Lisa Brook

Supported by The Work-Life Balance Trust 2003

Listening and responding to young people

Contents

Many adults, particularly parents – wrongly believe they know what young people worry about. However, any good researcher goes direct to the source. What the Young Voice organisation does is listen to the young and that is why I originally approached it. As Founder President of the Work-Life Balance Trust (an independent charity with no political affiliations) I know that Work-Life balance is a major concern for young people. Indeed as this survey shows, they want information on this issue more than on sex drugs or money.

It was because of this that I invited Adrienne Katz, Chief Executive of Young Voice to speak at The Savoy Hotel during Work Life Balance Week 2002.

Young people are not only important as individuals, they are the next British workforce and will share the burden of running this country while earning and paying the pensions of those who have already done their bit.

But the transition from school to workplace is tough enough, without the added stress of a young worker finding that he or she has neither the time nor energy to do anything BUT work. Such a situation can lead to stress which currently costs the NHS £2 billion per year.

It is the responsibility of today's adults – US - to ensure that we do not force our children into working environments that leave no time for family and community commitments or exercise; no time for further study or to pursue other personal interests whether these be raising goldfish or children.

Globalisation means that the economy now operates 7 days a week 24 hours a day. This brings pressure to bear on a workforce that is no longer confident of job security or an adequate pension and is already stretched to the limit by mergers acquisitions, down-sizing, out sourcing, new technology and the speed of innovation. The result is unprecedented and damaging stress to adults with knock-on stress to children, as the voices in this book testify.

This is why Britain needs to rethink and redesign workplaces and practices often dating from the 19th Century. What is needed is recognition that the way that people run their lives today need not penalise employers. Work-Life balance systems involve the adjustment of working patterns so that everyone – regardless of age, race or gender – can more easily combine work with their home responsibilities and interests.

Can Britain afford this? Yes. Research shows that the implementation of such systems attracts the best workers and reduces absenteeism while increasing retention of activity and profit. Nevertheless many employers are not yet convinced.

The aim of the Trust is to reconcile out-dated work practices with modern life patterns and responsibilities. Our approach is pro-active. Our first considerations are practicality and the business case.

This year our specific aim is to increase awareness of stress on young people and schoolchildren and to discover what might be done to prevent this. Will our kids look at us – especially their mothers – and say 'I don't want that life! In fact I don't want my own kids because life is tough enough to manage without them'?

This isn't a difficult aim. It is a logical, realistic, productive goal and one which we cannot afford to ignore – for the sake of the next generation of Young Voices.

Shirley Conran
Founder President Work-Life Balance Trust

Part One:
The Evidence

"...You've got to handle the stress, it's a teenage thing. The teenage disease yeah... but there's not a lot they can do. It's down to you and you've got to cope with it."

A young man of 17, talking to Young Voice in Waltham Forest, London.

The young man who so aptly described stress as a teenage disease was among more than a thousand young people who were sharing their experiences with Young Voice in a survey on health in 2002. Stress was their overriding issue and they complained that adults do little to help them cope.

60% of young people said they needed to be taught or shown more on how to cope with stress: this was higher than the number who wanted to be taught more on how to handle sex, money or drugs[1]. Stress it seems, is the most overlooked subject in the overcrowded curriculum.

'Work–Life Balance' has until now been linked with adults at work. The battle has been to get the world of work to recognize that workers are people too and that they will work better and remain in their jobs longer if they have some balance in their lives. The term has often referred to parents who are trying to balance work and family life, and it has scooped up in its wake workers who are not parents, but who may want a life or a career break.

---

1 'Wassup? Young people talk about health'. By Young Voice 2002, for Waltham Forest & Redbridge Youth Rising project. 1032 13-26 yr olds were surveyed, plus 4 drama workshops and 104 consultations.

Now young people are saying they need a balance in their lives too. They argue that not only are their own lives increasingly stressful with greater demands on them, but that living with stressed out adults is tough. Over a third of teenagers surveyed were worried about their mother's health, and almost one in five worried that their Mum was overly stressed.

Teenagers describe pressure from parents and from schools wanting to shine in the league tables. As tuition fees loom, some also have part time jobs, or care for a relative while doing 'A' levels. There are teenagers acting like parents for siblings, helping out while Mum's at work, interpreting for parents who don't speak good English, and coping with their parents' divorce. Alongside all this they feel the pressure to look good, keep up with fashion, be good friends to their mates, see granny and do some exercise. Boyfriend and girlfriend problems feel acute. In rural areas and crowded cities the effort of getting to and from college can add enormously to the workload.

One 17 year old studied by researchers Pat Allatt and Carolyn Dixon, in a rural isolated area, clocked up a 68.5 hour working week between lessons, homework, paid work and travel.[2] A speaker from that study describes the tension between school work, paid work and having a life as a teenager:

"A couple of girls in my English class the other day were crying because of the amount of work they'd got on. They were really stressed out. And a couple of people have two jobs you know, to support themselves through it. And I mean... I know you should make sacrifices and things, but you're still meant to go out and enjoy yourself aren't you, in your teenager years?"

Mandy, 17 years old in full time A level studies at FE College Spring 2000.

2 Allatt, P & Dixon, C. (2001) 'Learning to Labour: How 17 year old A'
   Level students manage part time jobs, full time study and other forms
   of work in times of rapid social change' Newsletter 4. Brighton ESRC
   Research Programme: Youth Citizenship and Social Change, 3- 6

But this level of stress is not only found in the A level years : A younger speaker told Young Voice:

"Every teenager – at certain stages, feels it's all getting too much with all you should be doing. Everyone expects so much of you. You think I'm gonna do well, I've got to get myself together, there is so much to do." 3

She is only thirteen years old.

Poor transport is a recognized stress for adult workers, but some teenagers travelled hours to college or to attend a group. In one case a teenage mother told us she travelled an hour and a half each way in the evening with her baby to attend the mother and baby group in a London borough. Students referred to a Pupil Referral Unit might travel as much as two hours to get there, because they no longer attend school locally.

But the role of stress in young people's lives goes unnoticed until there is a problem. They are seldom taught or shown how to handle it despite the fact that it is often linked to behaviour problems, depression, bullying and some serious illnesses. When they enter the workforce, being able to cope well under stress might be a skill employers would value, but it is usually ignored at school.

3 Katz, A. Buchanan, A & ten Brinke, J. 1997, Can Do Girls, Young Voice, London

There is growing agreement from researchers[4] that stress is increasing as signs of distress in young people mount up. But if you are a teenager you might be more concerned with your life now - than whether or not things are more stressful for teenagers these days.

Things can seem suddenly overwhelming. Different problems pile up so that what seemed manageable is suddenly no longer tolerable. All it takes is one argument with a girlfriend or boyfriend, one more row at home, or incident on the way to school and the dam bursts.

This little book hopes to draw attention to the problem and to give ideas about how to help at home and in classrooms, youth clubs and among groups of friends.

"A lot of boys on the outside seem perfectly OK, but inside are falling apart."

young man speaking in 'Leading lads' 1997 Young Voice

" Having two homes is like putting your life into two carrier bags every week"

Selina 16. 'Parent Problems!'

4. McNamara, S. (2000) 'Stress in Young People' Continuum. Bright Futures: Promoting Children and Young People's Mental Health 1999, Mental Health Foundation, Winefirld, A. & Tiggemann, M. Psychological distress, work attitudes and intended year of leaving school. Journal of Adolescence 16 p57-74

Stress related absence costs the UK £7 billion a year.[5]

Growing up in a stressed society

Growing up in a stressed society

40% of people in Britain think they are more stressed than five years ago according to a Mori poll for The Samaritans taken in April 2003. And younger people in our population are more stressed than the rest of us: Over half of those aged 15 –34 say they are more stressed than they were five years ago. The aim of this Samaritans' programme is to look at an emotional barometer of the nation and work towards better ways of handling stress and distress. They found that:

One in five Britons say they get 'very stressed out' at least once a day. This is more evident among workers: 23% of people working full time get stressed every day, compared to just 16% of those who aren't working.

Our society is particularly hard on parents and children. Around a third of parents said they get 'very stressed out' every day. This puts an unseen strain on children. But of all the age groups looked at in this poll, young people are the most stressed out on a daily basis: 24% of those aged 15 - 24 get wound up every day.

The Costs of stress

30% of sick leave is related to stress, anxiety and depression.[5]

Stress related employee absence is £530 per year per employee for small businesses and £545 for larger ones.[6] (CBI 1999)

Professor Carey Cooper of The School of Management UMIST reports that stress, depression and anxiety related illness costs the economy 5% – 10% of GNP annually.[7]

'45% of the workforce work in excess of working hours with major rises in damage to health, relationships and children's well-being and lowered productivity.' [8]

A company of 1000 employees can expect up to 300 people every year to suffer from depression and anxiety related illness with one suicide every decade.' [9]

5. Chartered Institute of Personnel and Development
6. BT Forum 1997
7. Confederation of British Industry Absence Survey 1999
8. Breakpoint/Breakthrough Work Life Strategies for the 21st century, Work Life Forum, 2000
9. Breakpoint/Breakthrough Report. The National Work Life Forum 2000

Has stress worsened?

Two in five people in Britain are more stressed than they were 5 years ago.[10]

Working days lost to stress/depression have risen from 6.5million (1995/96) to 13.5 million in 2001/02.[11]

Average annual days lost per case was 16 in 1995/96 rising to 29.3 in 2001/02.[12]

Researchers tend to agree that stress has risen in young people in recent decades.[13]

There have been increased referral rates of young people to in-patient Child & Adolescent Mental Health Services, including increases in emergencies.[14]

Stress and related conditions have doubled since 1990.

Health & Safety Executive Self-Reported Work Related Illness 2001/02: Results from a Household Survey SW101/02

Some teenagers have extra stress loads.

Family Life

There is a huge shift in the way that families live today, and increasing numbers of children are worried about, or living through their parents splitting up. They say that conflict at home is their second most frequent cause of stress after schoolwork. Some are navigating a balancing act between two homes, trying not to favour one parent over another. Damping down their own feelings can make some feel unexplained anger which they have to deal with.

"My anger gets cooped up inside and so I blurt it all out..."

Thomas aged 11 on coping with his parents' divorce.

'Parent Problems!' Young Voice 2000

10. Stress and Society - Samaritans MORI 2003
11. Samaritans MORI 2003
12. Health & Safety Executive Self-Reported Work Related Illness 2001/02: Results from a Household Survey SW101/02
13. McNamara, S. (2000) Stress in Young People Continuum, Bright

Futures: Promoting Children and Young People's Mental Health 1999, Mental Health Foundation, Winefird, A. & Tiggemann, M. Psychological distress, work attitudes and intended year of leaving school. Journal of Adolescence 16 p57-74
14. Street, C. Svanberg, J. (2003) Where Next? Young Minds

"It was awful at the start. I took on...not the mother role – but I used to make the tea and everything. And Dad was depressed, taking medicines. He used to sit in the chair and just look out of the window. If you knew my Dad that's just not like him. He's the most jokey kind of, you know, happy man. He went weird...I was only young. It wasn't fair."

Selina 16
Bren Neale & Amanda Wade.
'Parent Problems!' 2000 Young Voice

"I have to swap houses every day but I feel under pressure not to say anything about changing it 'cos Mum and Dad would probably go mental. They'd fight over every day. They argue over, like whoever has one long day. It's just relentless. I wish they would stop it I suppose." *Matt 14.*

Bren Neale & Amanda Wade. 'Parent Problems!' 2000 Young Voice

For a hidden minority violence is a part of family life:

"What's it like living in my family? It's horrible, because people hit people. I wish that we could have got on better." *Pete, 8* 'Parent Problems!'

"We moved to three different refuges, I'd have to make new friends...she said I'd have to change school...I'd been there since nursery...We weren't allowed to take a lot of stuff with us because she said we'd be moving around a lot."

Anjali, 10 - Mullender A. et al. 'Stop hitting Mum!' Young Voice 2003

Caring for parents

The number of carers under 18 has increased three fold since 1996. The 2001 Census revealed 149,000 compared to a 1996 figure of 51,000. An army of unseen young people hold the fort at home like this 12 year old girl:

"There are four children in our family. My brother's got dyspraxia. I've got a brother of 8, he's got asthma, a sister of 6 another brother of 14 and I'm 12. I help with the washing up and I help my Mum. My brother sometimes helps when I'm ill. My Dad normally helps in the morning when we're asleep. He goes at 7 a.m. and is back at 6 p.m.. My Nan takes the younger ones to school and fetches them back. Mum's physically disabled, she was really ill yesterday. The weekends are when I'm really busy. When I'm not well and the others have gone to school and I've still got to look after her its' really hard. She sometimes doesn't tell me what's going on. My Mum goes shopping with me in the wheelchair to Asda.

When Mum was in hospital Dad tried to cook but burnt the toast. I microwaved the baked beans. The doctor doesn't talk to me about how I am."

Young carers argue that their responsibilities are not recognized:

"I'd like to make a 'phone call home from school. I do sometimes at break times but I'd like to phone home every two hours."

Petty rules can stand in the way of a child checking on a problem at home. Some get so worried that they don't go to school if they think their parent is very ill that day. Attendance would rise if they could stay in contact, as any adult in the workplace might do with a mobile 'phone. Absence means a work backlog and more stress. These young people are caring for others but who is caring for them?

Looked after young people

Young people in care report very high stress levels, possibly moving to as many as three placements with foster carers in one year. This can mean repeatedly pulling up roots, friends, school and everything familiar including your social worker.

Homeless

Homeless young people aged 16-17 face the possibility of fixed penalty notices in a new white paper on antisocial behaviour. They may have experienced combinations of serious family disruption, physical or sexual abuse, local authority care or exclusion from school.

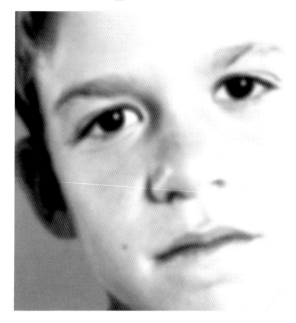

"I've been sexually abused, physically and verbally, I have never had anyone listen to me. I've had eight social workers and I get attached to them, then they're taken away from me. Somebody should have listened when the problems first started." *Female 15*

Children of prisoners and children who are prisoners.

The prison population in England and Wales has soared over the past two years and with it the number of children who are affected. It is estimated that as many as 140,000 children have a relative inside. Arrangements for their care are often ad hoc informal plans made at the last minute. Few of them have any say and they are not subject to the safety checks that would be in place were they adopted formally or placed in care. Legally ambiguous arrangements with neighbours are one example, another is an informal family arrangement. But the prison population is known to report high levels of abuse and mental disorder in their background, so many of these children find themselves in the very same abusive family situation from which their parent emerged.

The imprisonment of a relative places untold strains and hardships on families and on top of this, children are not always told the truth about the absent parent – some believe they have been abandoned, while others are told to keep it secret lest the family be shamed. The nature of the crime has an effect on the entire family. 11,000 prisoners were held more than 100 miles from home and 25,000 more than 50 miles, making visiting a gruelling and exhausting experience for their children. On the other hand some prison parents don't want their child to see them in there. The parent or relative caring for the child on the outside may be so traumatized he or she may not offer dependable parenting:

"Mum used to sit in a chair in the corner of the living room and just stare at the walls for ages... Seeing it in the paper didn't help... I didn't get to see my Dad until about six months after he'd gone to prison. Walking off from him after the visit was the hardest thing."

K. 16 'Parenting Under Pressure: Prison' Young Voice 2002

95% of young offenders in prison have a diagnosable mental illness or substance abuse problem.[20]

Vulnerable groups

59,000 young people live in care in the UK[15] 67% of those in care suffer with psychiatric disorders.[16]

37% of young offenders come from a care home.[17]

Up to half a million children and young people (5 per cent of the school population) have experienced the imprisonment of their father before leaving school[18], this may affect up to 140,000 children each year.[19]

Bullying is the most common reason for calls to Childline and has been for the past 5 years.

At least 16 children commit suicide every year due to bullying.[21]

University students are more stressed than non-students. 43% males/ 64% females report clinical anxiety with clinical depression in 12% and 15% respectively.[22]

Chaotic struggling families and periods in care also feature in the lives of young people who are in prison. These children have often experienced every form of exclusion, have poor mental and emotional health and are seldom equipped to cope upon release.

15. Coleman, J. & Scholfeild, J. (2003) Key data On Adolescence Trust For the Study of Adolescence
16. Bright Futures: Promoting Children and Young people's Futures 1999, Mental Health Foundation UK
17. HM Prisons Inspectorate
18. Dibb, L. 'Supporting Prisoners Children in School Project' Federation of Prisoners' Family Support group
19. Gampell, L. (1999) 'Response to the Government Consultation Document 'Supporting Families', Federation of prisoners' Family Support Groups
20. Hodgkin, R. (2002) Rethinking Child Imprisonment CRAE
21. Marr, N. & Field, T. (2001) 'Bullycide-Death at Playtime: An exposes of child suicide caused by bullying' Success Unlimited
22. Fox, P. Caraher, M. & Baker, H. (2001) 'Promoting Student mental Health' Vol2, issue Mental Health Foundation

Victims of racism and bullying :

Since September 11th, there has been a rise in racism and bullying among teenagers who reflect the society around them. In one inner London borough one third of young people from ethnic minority communities had been bullied for their religion in the three months immediately afterwards. But bullying is always a major cause of stress for each one of those who are targeted – and they show their stress in ways which are not always safe. Bullied teenagers became depressed or sometimes violent in their turn. They tend to seek protection, occasionally by joining a gang or by carrying a weapon. Some took a drug or alcohol to escape the tyranny of the bullying.

Bullying is one of the most common reasons for depression that school children described. Despite anti-bullying policies in schools, it is still prevalent. Bullying thrives on the journey to school, on buses, in the neighbourhood and on estates.

It is secretive, subtle and ever-changing like a virus.

Racism takes forms that reflect stereotypes and fears:

"I'm not being funny or anything – but they hang on to their bags 'cos I'm black."

14 year old girl, Hackney, London.

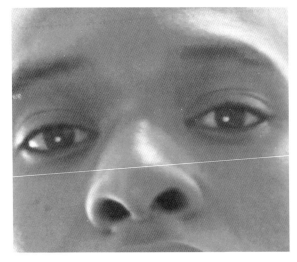

"Someone will come up to you at the shops and say, 'Where are you from?' You don't mind saying you're Asian - I'm proud of it...but it's that it's always on the agenda, never goes away." *Muslim Girl in Bradford, 18*

"Where the school is I don't feel safe. There is eggs and stones thrown at the bus."

Jewish boy in North London.

25% of our under 16 population are from minority communities and too many face discrimination or harassment.

All interviewed by Young Voice
1.   Play: The Verdict 2003 by Young Voice for The Children's Society
2.   'Thwarted Dreams - Young Views from Bradford' Young Voice 2003
3.   'Young Barnet Connects' Young Voice 2003

Just over a third of young people got 'a little' advice or teaching on how to handle stress. 27% said they did not get any help on coping with stress at all, while 22% said they got some advice, but it came too late. By the time they were in the workplace this was more marked still: Almost half of the young people who were already in jobs said they hadn't had any help with coping.

Only 17% were satisfied with the way they'd been taught or shown how to cope with stress.
'Wassup?' Young Voice 2002

Living with both parents or one made little difference but there was a difference between the sexes, girls were more likely than boys to say they'd been offered advice too late.

Where they live

Causes of stress and ways to relieve it can vary depending on where people live. While some teenagers feel safe and have opportunities to socialize and relax, for others life in towns and cities means fears and experiences of muggings, phone theft, vandalism and traffic problems. Teenagers hang out in the ramps in estates, complain of derelict playing fields and being seen as a threat by adults if they're in a group. But there is generally far more to do in towns and cities and more routes to get help or join a youth club, get entertainment or do sport.

On the other hand young people in villages raise different issues. Everyone knows them, there is little or no provision for young people and they hang out in the bus shelters or at the pub and in some cases public toilets. They have little chance of accessing services in confidence unless they can get to a town or use the internet. Lack of transport can be a major barrier. When asked where she hangs out after school and at weekends one young woman said:

"We go down to the bus shelter normally. I have to walk through sheep's droppings, we live up on the moors. The boys think it's cool to vandalise, like the bus timetable. The bus times are really important to us se we can go out and socialize." *Female 13*

16

Education is moving inexorably towards the independent learner- people make choices, and become responsible for their own learning. So young people are seen as having to stand on their own two feet without the emotional skills to do it. The changes in the curriculum have produced more testing and more stress.

"It's hard to unwind. Teachers try to make it better by saying it's got worse and that it wasn't as bad when they went through it, but again they're just guessing."

Male 14, Waltham Forest, London

"Last few months I got stressed...I had so much to do in so little time...at college I'm stressed 24/7 so much to do. I got 4 A-levels. The college doesn't advise you too much. In my tutorial we study key Skills and that's like another subject, so you don't get time to talk about stuff like stress."

Male 16, Waltham Forest, London.

17

Who felt they'd been failed?

Young people with special problems tended to feel they'd been failed by not learning to handle stress. This was more obvious among teenagers who said they were 'often depressed' or had been bullied, or if they rated their own stress levels as particularly high.

Every young respondent in the 'Wassup?' survey was asked to rate their own stress on a scale of 1-5, saying how they felt most of the time. One in five, or 231 individuals out of all the 1036 young people had scores at or near the top of the scale at 4 or 5. These stressed teenagers reveal their lack of strategies for stress.

40% said the help they'd got on coping had come too late.

39% said they hadn't received any teaching on this at all.

That suggests that more than three quarters of the most stressed teenagers either had no help with stress or it came too late. More than half of this stressed out group say they often feel depressed.

"I don't know where government money is going, they can't even find a cure for PMT and women have been having periods from the beginning of time" *Female 13 'Wassup?'*

Endangered and vulnerable

In a different study of 'At risk' young people and what they do when they feel very stressed: Young Voice found that compared to others, the young people considered 'at risk'[23] were more than three times as likely to smash something up when very stressed. They were three times as likely to drink alcohol and twice as likely to use an illegal drug. They were four times as likely to pick fights when very stressed. One quarter said 'Where I live' is a cause of stress and nearly a third said another cause was 'people with weapons'.

The ways in which these 'at risk' young people react make a powerful argument for teaching a menu of stress coping skills.

23. To be considered 'at risk' a young person had to answer positively to two or more of the following questions or statements: Use drug other than Cannabis in last month, Gang member, carry a weapon, smash things up or pick fights when distressed, feel depressed 'often' have suicidal thoughts or have made an attempt. Bully other people.

The Impact on Mental Health

It is generally agreed that around 20% of young people have mental health problems. Approximately –10% of these are severe.[24] Self-harm is of increasing concern.
In a recent Young Voice survey of 13-25 year olds, 18% feel depressed 'often', 8% had suicidal thoughts and 11% had made an attempt. 22% rated their stress levels as unbearably high most of the time.[25]

It is a government target to reduce suicides among young men as this tragic marker of a nation's health has been a cause of concern for the last few years.[26]

Impact on families

There is an:

Impact on the parent's relationship

Impact on the child who worries about parents

Impact on the child of a lack of support

Impact on other people, as the child may become a bully, a target or in other ways act out his or her distress.

Impact on a child's learning when either the parent or the child is stressed..

Stress and depression

45% of those who felt stressed have been depressed as a result.

1 in 5 people in Britain experience stress every day, of people feel isolated due to this; nearly all feel depressed and 1 in 8 have nowhere to turn. (*Samaritans poll on Stress.*)

Within a secondary school with 1000 pupils there are likely to be:

50 pupils who are seriously depressed

100 pupils who are suffering significant distress

5 to 10 girls who have an eating disorder

10 to 20 pupils with an obsessive compulsive disorder (*Young Minds*)

An estimated 156,000 young people between 5 and 16 make serious attempts to harm themselves each year.

Suicide accounts for over 1 in 5 of all deaths of young people aged 15 - 26

24. Young Minds figures
25. Wassup? David Stockdale, & Adrienne Katz for Waltham Forest & Redbridge 'Youth Rising'.programme 2002.

26. In 2001 the ONS published a study that suggested that 156,000 young people between 5 and 16 make serious attempts to harm themselves each year. (Source: Samaritans information pack 2001).
Suicide accounts for over a fifth of all deaths of young people aged 15-24 (the equivalent of two a day in the UK and republic of Ireland).

While worry about schoolwork hung like a heavy cloud over most of the young people, some were clearly coping with it better than others and levels of support were strikingly different. Some people thrive on pressure.

A short defined period of pressure was a good thing in some ways – the adrenalin and deadlines helped some people to perform at their best. But too many said they felt overwhelmed, and that the pressure was relentless, especially for those with additional problems.

For them, this overriding pressure of schoolwork could not simply be dealt with from a supportive family life because they had other worries that were greater than schoolwork. We have shown some causes of stress that were beyond the control of the individual young person – like parents' divorcing or a relative in prison. Bullying was another common problem over which they felt they had little control. Feeling powerless, was itself a cause of stress for young people. But here we explore worries about the health of someone close to you. Because the teenage years are so focused on changes within your own body, and adolescents are bombarded by 'health' messages about drugs and sex by adults, they seem suddenly more aware about health in others.

After schoolwork, conflict at home was the second most frequently mentioned cause of stress for young people.
Young Voice surveys 2001/2002

"I got really upset and freaked out with the situation at home so mum took me to the doctors. Then we all went to this therapy thing. I had to sit there with my mum and step-dad. I couldn't really talk in front of them...I needed someone to talk to by myself." *Charlie 14, 'Parent Problems!'*

Health - Invincible until they are teenagers?

Although children tend to feel invincible, in their teens they begin to worry about the health of people close to them; their parents, siblings, elderly relatives and close friends. At the same time, puberty brings a crisis to many who begin to find they are taunted and bullied with homophobic insults or tortured by bullies about their appearance or lack of height. Now is the time when worry about 'How I look' [27] becomes a painful reality. By the age of 14-15, more than one quarter of the whole sample of both sexes often worry about their own health which is sometimes a euphemism for 'am I developing normally?' In two single sex Young Voice studies, two thirds of girls at age 14 worry 'Am I fat?' and 46% of 14 year old boys in their turn, worry about 'How I look'. By the age of 15, fully half the boys say 'How I look' is a cause of stress.

High stress levels

Teenagers with the highest stress rating worry more than everyone else:

31% worry about their own health.

32% say 'I'm overly stressed'.

26% say 'I'm worried about my own depression' (compared to 11% of all others)

39% 'often' worry about their Mum's health

18% worry about Mum being frequently ill and 12% about her ongoing illness.

14% worry about their Mum's depression

25% worry their Mum is overly stressed

29% worry about the health of another relative

19% worry 'I am too thin or too fat'. [28]

Over a third of all teenagers said they worried about their mother's health. The most common reason given overall, was that she is overly stressed. There were links between Mum's health and stress and young people's own stress levels. These figures suggest that not only do teenagers worry about their mothers in this way, but if she is too stressed, ill or depressed, they lose out on the support from Mum that they look for. The most common cause of worrying about Dad healthwise, was smoking – but only 59% of young people who took part in this project lived with both parents. When violence is present it becomes the overwhelming stress eclipsing everything and raising the worries about mothers.

27 'Can-do Girls' Young Voice 1998' and 'Leading Lads' Young Voice 1999

28. 'Wassup?' Young Voice 2002

A link between worry about Mum's stress and their own behaviour?

Although almost one in five of all teenagers worry that Mum is overstressed, some were strikingly more worried about this than others: teenagers who carried a weapon, drug users, those in trouble with the police, and those who were stressed themselves were especially likely to say their own mother was overly stressed or depressed.

When Mum is not available to talk to you about health.

For the majority of teenagers, mothers are the most commonly consulted source of information on health issues. (She is also the person they turn to for emotional support above everyone else). But some groups of young people could not turn to their Mums for this help. When she is a newcomer to the UK and struggling with language and culture change, or ill herself, the teenager might be the translator – the go-between for mother and doctor. Mothers said that in these situations the parent and child had swapped roles, their teenager might know all a mother's private case notes – or have to ask the doctor questions on behalf of their mothers. Mothers in Bradford[29] who were consulted over several months, said they keenly felt the loss of their mothering role when this happened.

This reversal also meant that young people from some minority communities tended to worry more about their mothers health than their peers. They often feel responsible for their Mum's health and stressed at school worrying about her.

In these pages, young people with extra responsibilities or problems have been the focus - but every young person is entitled to support and understanding, however trivial he or she may think the problem is.

29. 'Thwarted Dreams, Young Views from Bradford'. Young Voice 2001

Are girls now more stressed than before?

Is stress always bad?

Are there different types of stress?

What makes a girl resilient?

What stresses girls out?

- Cause no 1 is worry over schoolwork named by 86%. Over half are 'often overwhelmed'
- Cause no 2 - Conflict at home
- Cause no 3 - Relationships outside the family
- 2/3 of girls worry about 'How I look'
- More than half worry about their parents
- Nearly half worry that parents work too hard
- Worry about parents splitting up
- PMS
- Acceptance by others
- Peer Pressure
- Drugs
- Getting pregnant
- Worries about getting a job
- Being followed or attacked
- Pressure to choose options/choices
- Am I normal?
- Feeling powerless
- Bullying
- Money
- Abuse

source: 'Can-Do Girls', Young Voice

The Perfect Girl?

Are we seeing greater levels of stress as girls achieve greater levels of success? It seems that girls are showing an increase in psychological distress while for boys it has remained fairly stable.

Research shows that some types of stress have risen in fifteen-year old girls. In two studies over a twelve-year period, the same measures of mental health were used. The results suggest that the types of stress that had risen over time were linked to: changes in family structure, changes in the transitions teenagers face, changes in the causes of stress such as exam pressure and changes in expectations about exam and career success.[30]

Some girls feel they must be perfect.[31] Whether in body size and image, ideal daughter, academic high achiever and best friend – girls are expected to do all these things well. They set themselves high standards. Parents are putting on pressure they say, and school expects them to do well to keep the league table rating high. While some level of stress can be a motivator, stress in all areas of life can be overwhelming. One issue is clearly a product of our time: Girls are watching their working mothers and see how stressed and exhausted they are.[32]

30. Fifteen, female and Stressed: Changing patterns of Psychological Distress over time. Patrick West & Helen Sweeting , Medical Research Council. 2003

31. Meeting at the Crossroads, Lyn Mikel Brown& Carol Gilligan, Ballantyne, New York

32 Can-do Girls, Adrienne Katz, Ann Buchanan, Young Voice.1998

Over 80% of girls would turn to their mother first for emotional support. The lack of this available supportive mum is felt keenly:

Young women speaking in Can Do Girls' Young Voice

"I worry that she's worrying about me so I don't tell her."

17 talking about her Mum.

"My parents work so hard, they're already stressed, I try to deal with it on my own."

"There is pressure on your appearance, magazines give the impression girls have to look good." *13.*

"Watching women around me it must be so difficult to balance work and kids. Both are always on your mind. You can't tell the children to go away, and work is becoming a total goal."

13 years female.

Girls

"Mostly girls influence you really. You have to dress like your friends- you need your friends otherwise you think, I'm going to be alone. This scares people. Nobody wants to be left out. It starts off with fashion conscious people who don't feel sure enough of the person they are anyway." *Girl, 13*

'Can Do Girls' Young Voice

Young women speaking in Can Do Girls' Young Voice

"A person with no cash for clothes can't quite fit in, they might feel like outcasts and alone. They'll do anything to fit it." *Girl, 13*

Over a third of girls in a study of 3000 [33] said their parents were anxious that they did well and 28% believe that parents put too much pressure on them. But most of the pressure was self imposed: 83% said they always set themselves high standards.

"I know I can cope. My parents expect a lot and I want to rise to their expectations myself." *Female, 17*

How can girls be shown that they are valued for themselves and not only for their achievements?

"I felt under a lot of pressure. In lower 6th I got 4 A's and the same in the mocks. For parents and teachers- they couldn't comprehend me not getting these A's. I was so intensely concerned to achieve something you know you can achieve. I knew that on the right day I could do it, But would it be the right day?" *Female, 18*

But it isn't acceptable to be too swotty:

"Girls might not seem so swotty if that's what the boy finds attractive." *Female, 13 years*

This might be another cause of stress.

33. 'Can-do Girls' 1997, Katz A. Young Voice

What do girls do when they feel very stressed?

They listen to music, talk to someone or stay in their room. Girls opt for staying in their room more than boys do. More than half listen to music to de-stress. Around a quarter get irritable and a similar number go out with their friends. Girls are half as likely as boys to do sport or exercise when they feel stressed, but equally likely to say they smash things and a little more likely to smoke. Similar levels of boys and girls say they use an illegal drug when they're stressed, or drink alcohol. One in five do nothing.

Wassup? 525 boys 511 girls 2002 Young Voice

Extra vulnerable

But girls who are more vulnerable had a different story to tell. Out of a sample of 2062 young people in inner London, we found 315 boys and girls who reported two or more difficulties. Boys were more likely to be in this situation than girls but for those 74 girls who were, their stories were worrying.

To make things worse, the girls 'at risk' said they took several risky actions when they were very stressed. Almost half of them feel depressed 'often'. They might be part of a gang, they fight and smash things – they say they are often depressed and 23 out of the 74 'at risk' girls say they've made a suicide attempt. Almost half of them say they are very stressed most of the time, and 25 of them have turned to drugs. 9 gave the reason for this as "To get rid of stress, and 8 said it was " To relieve depression."

Problems pile up.

Half of these 'at risk' girls said conflict at home was making them stressed, they tended to have boyfriend problems (46%) money difficulties (41%) and more than a quarter had parents who were separating (26). Nearly one in five said racism was causing them stress (19%) with bullying listed by more than a quarter (28%).

41% of these young women said that a cause of stress was being shouted at and more than half found relationships with friends to be stressful.

Overwhelmingly 80% found schoolwork to be a major cause of stress. Their lives were stress filled and the way they coped or responded to these stresses was endangering them and often the people around them.

The figures above were taken from a study called Fitting in or Fighting Back. Young Voice 2002

While we are focusing on young people with special problems in these pages, it is vital to remember that most young women are coping very well with their lives especially when they have good support at home and close friends. That is why the extra vulnerable girls stand out in sharp contrast.
What they tell us serves as a wake up call – to help prevent others from slipping into these crises.

The highest rate of self-harm is found among 13-15 year old girls.

(Survey ONS 'Children and Adolescents who try to harm, hurt or kill themselves)

What stresses boys out?

- Schoolwork and exams
- Conflict at home.
- Money
- People with weapons
- Relationships with friends
- Being shouted at
- My health
- Bullying
- Worries about a job
- Parents separating
- Drugs
- Hospital appointments
- Being Hit; fear of being attacked
- People carrying weapons,
- Racism
- Abuse
- Being forced to do things against your will
- Am I normal?
- Feeling powerless
- Failure at sport

What boys have to say

'I could talk to my Dad, but he's always at work and I don't see him on my own much.'

'My Dad wants to be proud of his son, so I can't tell him my life's a mess.'

'You can't show any emotion, it'll be seen as weak ...you get picked on if you show your weakness.'

'The one thing I'd say could improve things for boys would be if they could get their thoughts out.'

'I wouldn't tell my mate how I felt – it's not that sort of friendship.'

Young Men talking in 'Leading lads' Young Voice

"I'm not comfortable speaking to the doctor - he's a bit dumb" *17, 'Wassup?'*

What do boys do when they're stressed?

43% listen to my music
32% talk to someone
32% stay in my room
25% keep it to myself
17% go out with friends
16% said they do 'nothing'
15% go out on my own
2% Use helpline/email service/counsellor

Less helpful reactions:

16% smash something up
11% smoke a cigarette
9% pick fights
8% use an illegal drug
7% drink alcohol
Feeling unsafe:
47% would carry a weapon 'for safety'
17% would join a gang,

'The one thing I'd say could improve things for boys would be if they could get their thoughts out.'

Extra vulnerable

241 boys from a total of 1223 were found to be 'at risk' their reactions to stress were very different from the average. They were 4 times as likely to drink alchohol, three times as likely to use an illegal drug, more than three times as likely to pick fights and more than three times as likely to smoke a cigarette. More than three times as many smash things up (50%).

High Stress

Although boys and girls differed in their responses to stress this was not as marked as the difference between the very stressed young people and everyone else.

Responses to stress – young people in the Wassup?
Sample 1036 people,

51% male 49% female

	Male	female	Very stressed
Talk to someone	29%	48%	37%
Stay in my room	26%	45%	51%
Get irritable	11%	23%	33%
Smash things	14%	16%	27%
Smoke cigarette	11%	13%	21%
Pick fights	9%	10%	22%
Illegal drugs	7%	6%	13%
Alcohol	7%	6%	14%
Call a helpline	2%	2%	3%

"Some boys can't talk about it - this is why musicians are so successful They articulate it for them - films and music" *18, London*

Making music can be a route to life skills. A project called Rithmik teaches those who like to DJ how to organise gigs, dealing with transport and insurance. By learning to plan, think ahead and make things happen, young men began to get a different view of themselves as capable, They are involved at all levels. They set up their own companies with websites and turn a hobby into a route towards a way to earn.

"It's giving me a challenge, that's what I like about it. Life's got to be challenge innit?" *Male, 16, Rithmik Barnet*

Boys described having a secret life - the inner self they never show. Through music and drama they are sometimes freed up to use the whole range of their personality.

Creative dramatherapy has been especially successful - in which young men worked towards finished products like plays, mini 'films', books, newspapers and photo displays[34] to express their feelings. This project was 'boy friendly' with the use of technology and equipment.

34 'Act Up Speak Out', Hull & East Riding Community Health NHS Trust.

Son, we're not like those parents who pressurise their kids. We won't feel any different about you if you've failed your exams, blown the chance of university, ruined your one shot at a decent job and messed up your life.

"I've been stressed with parents pushing you, they want you to do good." *Male 16*

Part two:
Tackling Stress

What worked for girls?

- "My parents listen to my problems and views"
- "They like me to make my own decisions"
- "They often talk about things that matter to me"
- Fairness – feeling you're being treated fairly and equally within the family.
- Consistency.
- Respect - a two-way thing.

"You don't want advice, you want someone to say, 'you make sense', not 'I can help you' - just be there." *'Can-do Girls' Young Voice.*

"Parents are the one reliable thing – you feel that at any time anywhere you can 'phone them and say 'I need help' and they'll come and get you."

What was less helpful?

- "Trying to control everything I do."
- "They put too much pressure on me."
- "Lots of arguing at home."
- "My parents take no notice of me".
- Physical punishment.
- Being unable to talk to mum
- Gender inequality at home

These are linked with:

- Low self-esteem
- Feeling powerless
- Depression
- Being bullied
- Losing interest in schoolwork
- Not taking care of self
- More susceptible to peer pressure

'Can do Girls' Young Voice.

Tackling Stress

What worked for boys?

Talking is not always the right strategy.

"I don't think people like telling others their problems. I think it makes it worse."

Young man talking in 'Leading Lads' 1997 Young Voice.

To someone just managing to hold himself together, the idea of talking about it and breaking down or making yourself vulnerable, can be unbearable. But there are other ways to build support and trust until help can be given. Young men might find getting information about the problem gives them a sense of control – or they may choose a helpline because in that situation it is confidential, they are in control and can put the telephone down if they want to. Young men are using email as an even more impersonal source of help and The Samaritans offers an email service. For some individuals, having warm and caring mates or family around simply 'accepting you as you are without asking questions' helps the most. Simon, who worked at a City farm for a while enjoyed the unquestioning love of the animals who depended on him. Later he was able to talk about it.

see page 30 for boys' comments

"Yeah, I just go to a search engine, put in like 'drugs' and it brings up information. It would be the first place I get information. I'm waiting for an e-mail back from this website." *16, 'Wassup?'*

What does resilience consist of?

- Being better prepared for reality. Our expectations adjusted.

- Being able to process information and make a decision.

- Being able to hold on to your self-image and values under pressure

- Feeling supported.

- Know when to get help and where.

- Self-esteem, sense of autonomy and ability to act.

"It is important for schools to treat every child as an individual. Teachers manage that- even at a large school like mine."

Young man talking in 'Leading Lads' 1999 Young Voice.

"The public image of boys having to be big and tough needs to be broken down- maybe like men burning their jockstraps!"

Young man speaking in 'Leading Lads' 1999 Young Voice

Below are some tips from boys and young men on how to help:

- Don't demand that a boy 'act like a man' by denying him understanding and support.
- Don't make academic success a competition between girls and boys.
- Recognise that how you feel affects how you learn.
- Teach pupils how to manage conflict and deal with anger.
- Give strategies for managing time and sudden work overloads.
- Encourage a sense of belonging and mutual respect.
- Try to remove the stigma of asking for help.
- Share activities that build a sense of safety within a team or group.
- Use role-play or drama to explore situations.
- Loosen the 'genderscript' that dictates how boys must behave.

Urge young men to seek help by emphasising that this involves manly characteristics such as:

- Courage
- Taking charge of your life
- It's a masculine thing to do rather than be powerless
- If you want to protect those closest to you and avoid putting your problems onto them – you can get help elsewhere.
- It's confidential if you use a helpline.

The most important things parents could do:

- "My parents listen to my problems and views"
- "They like me to make my own decisions"
- "They often talk about things that matter to me"
- Fairness – feeling you're being treated fairly and equally within the family.
- Be consistent.
- Respect - a two way thing.
- Dad spends time with me.

What was not helpful for boys:

- "Trying to control everything I do."
- "They put too much pressure on me."
- "Lots of arguing at home."
- "My parents take no notice of me".
- Physical punishment.
- Unable to talk to Mum.
- Expected to deal with problems alone

These situations were linked to:

- Low self-esteem
- Feeling powerless
- Depression
- Being bullied
- Losing interest in schoolwork
- Not taking care of self
- More susceptible to peer pressure

'Leading Lads' Young Voice 1999.

Questions for parents to think about

- Is all stress bad?
- What is democratic parenting?
- How do you handle your own stress?
- What tools can you teach?
- Do you notice signs of stress early enough?
- Are you unconsciously piling on the pressure?
- Humour helps! How can you use it?

Can you help address practical problems?

"I don't have anywhere quiet to revise. If there was somewhere, that would help 'cos I would do the work and then would have nothing to stress about." *Male 15*

"Before, my parents tried to push me too much. I dealt with it by showing my parents my grades...I explained to them I needed space and if they kept stressing me it was going to make me do worse not better and they understood and left me alone. If I have any problems I ask them" *Male 16, 'Wassup?'*

Help your child keep up energy levels:

"Once you get into them exams it's like a nightmare they're all bunched together." *20.*

"Yeah I do (get stressed) – exams – I hate them so much, when I do an exam I start shaking. I hate it so much. I shake 'cos of nerves. The teachers make it worse the way they talk to us, saying no noise and no talking, you know that anyway. If they said it in a good way, but they say it in a bad way and I get scared." *Male 14.*

Tip: Learn some breathing and relaxation techniques together

If a young person asks you for help...

- Avoid the pitfalls!
- Don't tell a story about your life and how you overcame this problem.
- Don't immediately give them the case story of someone else.
- Don't say 'If I were you...'
- Acknowledge that this person is unique – don't stereotype them because you've met this problem before.
- Can you listen effectively?
- What are their options? How do they see the difficulty and which of the options have they explored? they may define the problem differently from the way you see it.
- Don't tell them what to do, but help them come to their own decision by weighing up the possibilities or identifying the problems.
- Don't cut them short before they've had their say – by interrupting and saying you know all about this problem even if you do so sympathetically.
- To make a decision young people need tools. They need to learn to consider options and consequences. You can't hurry this and they may take the wrong decision, if they have sound reasons for doing so. We all have to live with our mistakes but better ours than someone else's.
- Some people are indecisive, nervous or cynical for a long period before making a decision to act.
- What about developing a plan to fall back on if things don't work out with the first idea?
- If you are not the parent but an outside supporter or advice giver, take notes and keep a record of your discussion, remind yourself of best practice and child protection protocols.
- Remember this young person has rights.
- Know the law or find out.*
- Can you avoid using trite and patronizing phrases, like 'When I was young...' or 'You don't want to do that'.

*'Is it legal?' Is a booklet obtainable from National Family & Parenting Institute.

Trust between the helper and the young person

For a helping service to work there has to be what is called a healing partnership. This means that there has to be trust and engagement between the two partners in this new relationship. The young person has to enter the partnership with a willingness to engage in the help. He or she may not be quite ready for this when you first talk. Someone who has had contact with several services and been passed from one to the other or assessed by each one, can feel that going to an appointment even if made by a trusted person, will do no good.

"I used to have a psychiatrist, he tried to get me into one (drug rehabilitation unit) 'cos I was on a Class A drug, but I never went."

Male 16

"You tell them the story of your life, and then they leave. They probably tell this geezer about your life over a pint." *male 17*

"They were rubbish, they (social services and A.R.T.) didn't help, they make you wait around for months then did nothing when you were in the system."

female 14, excluded from school.

Or perhaps they see the helping person as powerless?

"I told my Mum about my problems, but she can't do nothing." *Male 11, being bullied.*

Try making sure that he or she remains the 'actor' – the one who takes action and makes the choices, unless the problem is too great or the teenager is in an acute state.

The helper acts as the sounding board enabling this to happen.

You provide the sympathy, guidance and help to get the information on which the decision is made. Sometimes a young person will load all their troubles onto the parent who will then be left worrying about the problem. The teenager may now feel free of it and while you are still worrying, they may have got past the crisis simply by sharing it with you. Avoid coming back on this problem too strongly next time you talk – feel them out gently, life can move on very quickly when you are 15 and there are those who don't want to be reminded of a vulnerable patch.

Simple ways to relax

Exercise

Take a bath

Try aromatherapy oils

Listen to music

Drink a calming herbal tea.

Write down the problem

Do some deep breathing exercises such as yoga

Meet up with friends

Get help from a confidential service – see list page 43

"Sharing problems is always something girls do."

17 year old female.

"The boys turn to the girls when they are upset and tell them their troubles. The girls would get hysterical without the calming effect of the boys in our house."

Female student in a house share at university.

Recognising signs of Anorexia

Fast weight loss

Eating less and less

Panicky feelings when faced with a big meal

Food in your thoughts all the time

Obsessing about your body size and weight compared to others,

Periods stopping or not starting in girls.

Feeling moody

Withdrawing from friends

Feeling cold

Trying to be perfect

Sleeping badly

Body hair growing

Throwing up a lot can cause problems with teeth.

Becoming secretive or pretending to eat with family members but not swallowing.

Binge eating and bulimia are other ways of using food to cope with painful feelings. Guilt and feeling bad about yourself can accompany binge eating. Then some people feel they must get rid of this food. They might feel that they hate themselves or that they have let themselves down. Swinging through these cycles of bingeing because they are upset and then feeling that they must punish themselves are typical signs of bulimia.

Like anorexia, this can lead to other problems like sleeping problems, infections, dehydration, bad teeth, changes in periods for girls and a feeling of helplessness and isolation.

What's the worst that can happen?

Challenging fear and stress: What if I fail my exams?

Chatbox 10 minutes
In pairs or small groups.

- What would be the worst thing that could happen?
- How likely is it really?
- How bad would that actually be?
- What would still be the same in my life?
- Could I try again later?
- Could I study something else?
- What would be the best thing that could happen?

" We need to have younger GP's. Maybe GP's who are still studying could go into youth centres so we don't feel intimidated"
16, Male 'Wassup?'

" I'm looking for ways to help my brother man, but like I said, if he don't want to help himself you're not going to be able to help him"
16, Male (Brother with drug problem) 'Wassup?'

Activity box in a group, 20 minutes

Each person has two 'Post its.' Each writes on one, the worst that could happen if they fail.

Each also writes on the second post it what would be the best thing that could happen if I fail my exams?

Gather these and group them on a chart putting similar types of ideas together.

Discuss with the group what these categories might be.

Now look at all of them together and see the most common fears and the most positive alternatives.

By seeing how many people feel the same way—an individual may feel less alone and more supported. By seeing unusual ideas some individuals are encouraged to think outside the box.

There are always a few humourists in the group and they too play an important role.

This activity allows the quietest people to join in without self exposure.

It allows some pupils to see that they are not at the worst level of worry.

On your own: What are my strengths?

Write down every skill you have from making friends to drawing. Include you life skills, like managing money, reading a map. Making jokes, heating baked beans....

Chatbox

How do I know if I need help?
Small groups or in pairs. 20 minutes

Brainstorm signs of stress and have the groups or pairs write these signs up on a flipchart.

Some of these might be:

Not able to sleep.

Not eating normally

Can't concentrate.

Irritable all the time,

Panic attacks.

Feeling exhausted all the time

Over energised

Picking fights and edgy

Headaches

Pressurised

Some of these signs may only happen occasionally, or several might be happening at once. If they last and lots come together, you may want to get help, or get help for a friend.

Depression

When we are depressed, it can affect our energy, our thinking, our emotions, our sleep, just like stress—but we can also feel we are worthless, guilty, without hope, unable to decide anything. Self-hatred or loss of interest in life generally can overtake us. We can feel we don't deserve anything and can't do anything.

In any case, everything seems such a huge effort. We can come to focus only on the problems and nothing else, we can see no way in which things could get better and feel nobody could help or possibly understand.

It takes courage and effort to get help, but it can make a difference. There are lots of places to get help listed at the back of this book. You can stay in control and calls to Samaritans and Childline are confidential.

Advice box

Identify the problem—what kind of solution is needed?

■ What is problem- focused coping?

This is when you try to find ways to manage a problem with practical solutions.

■ What is emotion- focused coping?

This is finding a way to feel better about the problem.

1. Talking with a partner can you suggest types of problems that fit into these two categories?

2. What sort of problems are you facing? Are they both types? Do you need different kinds of help?

Some problems are long term and not in your power to change, like an illness in a close relative. Perhaps the best action you can take might be:

■ Caring for yourself in order to survive and manage the problem:

Relaxation

Taking time out

Treats

Exercise

Time with supportive friends

Manage your time.

Take stock from time to time.

Getting better informed – know the facts.

Find out where to get help in case you need it.

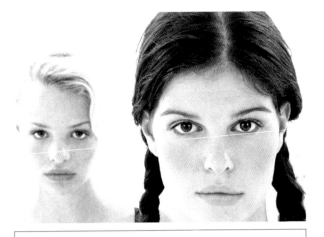

Activity to do alone or with a friend.

Challenge the impossible yardsticks you set yourself:

Who says ?

I have to do well all the time.

I have to look good always.

I have to be a good friend always.

Boys must deal with problems themselves.

I have to make my parents proud of me.

I have to do everything.

I have to win.

I have to take it because I want a friend.

Ideas to do on your own

Think about your options:

- Are there different types of stress?

- Is stress always bad?

- Some stress motivates, can you use stress in a positive way?

What do you do when you feel very distressed?

- Does this make you feel better or worse?

- Some people take steps that make their problems worse. Can you think of any steps which might do this?

- Sometimes the actions people take put them or other people in danger. What sort of steps might seem like a solution but are in fact dangerous?

- Have you ever taken some steps that have helped you or a friend?

- Have you ever felt you wished someone would take steps to help you? What sort of things would you have liked them to do?

Young Minds helpline for parents
0800 0182138
www.youngminds.org.uk

and

Parentline 0808 8002222

Where do you turn for help when you feel very stressed?

Fill in your web of support.
You are in the centre, the next circle are those who are closest to you, like family and friends, the next circle might be teachers, sports coaches, other people you know and trust. The outside circle might be help lines, services or any other place you could turn to for help.

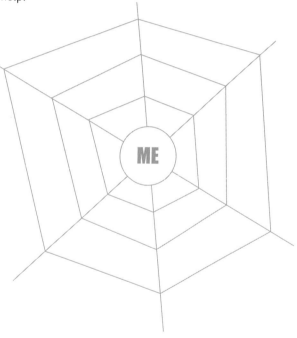

Childline

Freepost NATN 1111
London E1 6BR
Tel 0800 1111 24 hours
Textphone 0800400222 www.childline.org.uk

Get Connected

Helping you connect to the right organisation for advice. Language line available for those who may require a translator.
Lines open every day 1pm – 11pm
0808 808 4994

Relate Line

confidential counselling for children young people and adults. Lines open Mon to Fri 9.30am – 4.30pm.
0845 130 4010

NHS Direct

www.nhsdirect.nhs.uk
24 hours confidential advice and information on health questions
0845 46 47

Children's Legal Centre

Advice line 01206 873820
Mon-Fri 10 am –12.30 am
Free legal advice on any issue
www.childrenslegalcentre.org

Carers UK

Mon-Fri 9 am - 5 pm
0207 490 8818

There 4 me

www.there4me.com
Website for 14-16 year olds –
on screen advice and agony aunt.

Youth Access

Where to go for counselling
Mon-Fri 9,00 am – 5 pm
0208 7729900
Email admin@youthaccess.org.uk

Eating Disorders Association

Mon-Fri 4 pm – 6.30 pm
Help and support.
0845 634 7650

NSPCC

Child protection Helpline 0808 8005000

NSPCC Asian freephone 11 am to 7 pm

Counselling information and advice.
0808 0967719

Cruse Bereavement care

Mon-Fri, 9.30 am –5 pm.
Helpline 0870 1671677

National Drugs Helpline

Free and confidential 0800 77 66 00 24 hrs

Samaritans

Confidential support
08457 90 90 90
email jo@samaritans.org

It's not your fault

www.itsnotyourfault.com
a website for children and teenagers whose parents are getting divorced.

"Give us the information we need about the real things that are happening in our lives"